ONE SMALL POSITIVE THOUGHT IN THE MORNING CAN CHANGE YOUR WHOLE DAY

An Inspirational Journal - Notebook to Write In

DATE: ___/___/___

"You were given this life because you are strong enough to live it!" - Unknown

never give up

DATE:___/___/___

think positive

"The best way to gain self-confidence is to do what you are afraid to do." – Unknown

DATE: ___/___/___

"Have dreams and dream big!
Dream without fear"

MAKE IT HAPPEN

DATE:___/___/___

think positive

"Believe in miracles but above all believe in yourself!"

DATE: ___/___/___

"Let your dreams be as big as your desire to succeed"

BELIEVE YOU CAN

DATE:___/___/___

think positive

"Never downgrade your dreams, reach for the stars and believe in your self power"

DATE:___/___/___

"They say I dream too big. I say they think too small" - Unknown

BELIEVE IN YOURSELF

DATE:___/___/___

think positive

"Never be afraid to start something new,
if you fail it is just temporary, if you believe and
persist you will succeed"

DATE: ___/___/___

"Your driving force and your power lies within you and the size of your dreams, never give up!"

TAKE ACTION!

DATE:___/___/___

think positive

"Wherever you go, go with all your heart." - Confucius

DATE:___/___/___

"Build your own dreams or you will end up building someone else's dreams"

never give up

DATE: ___/___/___

think positive

"Your dreams and your goals are the seeds of your own success"

DATE:___/___/___

"Never give up, keep going no matter what!"

MAKE IT HAPPEN

DATE:___/___/___

think positive

"Start where you are and take chances"

DATE: ___/___/___

"If you never give up you become unbeatable, just keep going!"

BELIEVE YOU CAN

DATE: ___/___/___

think positive

"Life isn't about finding yourself. Life is about creating yourself."
- George Bernard Shaw

DATE: ___/___/___

"Keep your motivation and your momentum with a new goal every day!"

BELIEVE IN YOURSELF

DATE:___/___/___

think positive

"Change your life today. Don't gamble on the future, act now, without delay." — Simone de Beauvoir

DATE: ___/___/___

"The person who says it cannot be done should not interrupt the person who is doing it." – Chinese Proverb

TAKE ACTION!

DATE: ___/___/___

think positive

"Aim for the stars to keep your dreams alive"

DATE: ___/___/___

"There are no limits to what you can Achieve if you believe in your dreams"

never give up

DATE:___/___/___

think positive

"When you feel you are defeated, just remember,
you have the power to move on, it is all in your mind"

DATE:___/___/___

"Don't just dream your dreams, make them happen!"

MAKE IT HAPPEN

DATE:___/___/___

think positive

"Opportunity comes to those who never give up"

DATE:___/___/___

"You are the creator of your own opportunities"

BELIEVE YOU CAN

DATE:___/___/___

think positive

""Always aim for bigger goals, they have the power to keep you motivated"

DATE:___/___/___

"Every achievement starts with a dream and a goal in mind"

BELIEVE IN YOURSELF

DATE:___/___/___

think positive

"Success is not a place or a destination,
it is a way of thinking while always
having a new goal in mind"

DATE: ___/___/___

"Fall seven times and stand up eight." –
Japanese Proverb

TAKE ACTION!

DATE:___/___/___

think positive

"Change the world one dream at a time,
believe in your dreams"

DATE: ___/___/___

"Dreams make things happen; nothing is impossible as long as you believe."

never give up

DATE:___/___/___

think positive

"Never loose confidence in your dreams,
there will be obstacles and defeats, but you will
always win if you persist"

DATE:___/___/___

"Dreams are the energy that power your life"

MAKE IT HAPPEN

DATE:___/___/___

think positive

"Never wait for someone else to validate your existence, you are the creator of your own destiny"

DATE: ___/___/___

"Always dream big and follow your heart"

BELIEVE YOU CAN

DATE:___/___/___

think positive

"Everything you dream is possible
as long as you believe in yourself"

DATE:___/___/___

"Never stop dreaming" - Anonymous

BELIEVE IN YOURSELF

DATE: ___/___/___

think positive

"A successful person is someone that understands temporary defeat as a learning process, never give up!"

DATE:___/___/___

"Dream big, it's the first step to success" - Anonymous

TAKE ACTION!

DATE:___/___/___

think positive

"Motivation comes from working on our dreams
and from taking action to achieve our goals"

DATE:___/___/___

"Dreams are the foundation to our imagination and success"

DATE: ___/___/___

think positive

*"Your mission in life should be to thrive
and not merely survive"*

DATE:___/___/___

"The right time to start something new is now"

MAKE IT HAPPEN

DATE:___/___/___

think positive

"Doing what you believe in, and going after your dreams will only result in success." - Anonymous

DATE: ___/___/___

"Be brave, fight for what you believe in and make your dreams a reality."

BELIEVE YOU CAN

DATE: ___/___/___

think positive

"The will to win, the desire to succeed, the urge to reach your full potential... these are the keys that will unlock the door to personal excellence." – Confucius

DATE:___/___/___

"Put more energy into your dreams than Into your fears and you will see positive results"

BELIEVE IN YOURSELF

DATE: ___/___/___

think positive

"Let your dreams be bigger than your fears and your actions louder than your words." - Anonymous

DATE:___/___/___

"Dream. Believe. Create. Succeed" - Anonymous

TAKE ACTION!

DATE: ___/___/___

think positive

"Start every day with a goal in mind and make it happen with your actions"

DATE:___/___/___

"You are never to old to set new goals and achieve them, keep on dreaming!"

DATE:___/___/___

think positive

"If you have big dreams you will always have big reasons to wake up every day"

DATE: ___/___/___

"To achieve our dreams we must first overcome our fear of failure"

MAKE IT HAPPEN

DATE:___/___/___

think positive

"Difficulties are nothing more than opportunities in disguise, keep on trying and you will succeed"

DATE:___/___/___

"Use failure as a motivation tool not as a sign of defeat"

BELIEVE YOU CAN

DATE: ___/___/___

think positive

"Always have a powerful reason to wake up every new morning, set goals and follow your dreams"

DATE:___/___/___

"Have faith in the future but above all in yourself"

BELIEVE IN YOURSELF

DATE: ___/___/___

think positive

"Never let your dreams die for fear of failure,
defeat is just temporary; your dreams are your power"

DATE: ___/___/___

"The secret of getting ahead is getting started." – Mark Twain

TAKE ACTION!

DATE:___/___/___

think positive

"A failure is a lesson, not a loss. It is a temporary and sometimes necessary detour, not a dead end"

DATE:___/___/___

"Your future is created by what you do today not tomorrow" - Anonymous

DATE:___/___/___

think positive

"Never let your doubt blind your goals, for your future lies in your ability, not your failure" — Anonymous

DATE:___/___/___

"Don't go into something to test the waters, go into things to make waves"
— Anonymous

MAKE IT HAPPEN

DATE:___/___/___

think positive

"Laughter is the shock absorber that softens and minimizes the bumps of life" — *Anonymous*

DATE: ___/___/___

"Dream – Believe – Achieve"

BELIEVE YOU CAN

DATE: ___/___/___

think positive

"Hope is a waking dream." – Aristotle

DATE:___/___/___

"I am never a failure until I begin blaming others" - Anonymous

BELIEVE IN YOURSELF

DATE: ___/___/___

think positive

"Never give up on a dream just because of the time it will take to accomplish it. The time will pass anyway."
– Anonymous

DATE:___/___/___

"Your only limitation is your imagination"
— Anonymous

TAKE ACTION!

DATE: ___/___/___

think positive

"If you want to feel rich, just count all the things you have that money can't buy" — Anonymous

DATE:___/___/___

"It does not matter how slowly you go as long as you do not stop" – Confucius

never give up

DATE:___/___/___

think positive

"Some pursue success and happiness – others create it" — Anonymous

DATE: ___/___/___

"A goal without a plan is just a wish." – Antoine de Saint-Exupery

MAKE IT HAPPEN

DATE: ___/___/___

think positive

"It's better to have an impossible dream than no dream at all." – Anonymous

DATE:___/___/___

"All things are possible if you believe"

BELIEVE YOU CAN

DATE:___/___/___

think positive

"The winner always has a plan; The loser always has an excuse" — Anonymous

DATE:___/___/___

"What consumes your mind, controls your life"

BELIEVE IN YOURSELF

DATE: ___/___/___

think positive

"There is no elevator to success.
You have to take the stairs" — Anonymous

DATE:___/___/___

"Never let defeat have the last word" — Anonymous

TAKE ACTION!

DATE:___/___/___

think positive

"Don't let yesterday's disappointments, overshadow tomorrow's achievements" — *Anonymous*

DATE:___/___/___

"Hope is a waking dream." – Aristotle

DATE: ___/___/___

think positive

"We are limited, not by our abilities, but by our vision"
— Anonymous

DATE: ___/___/___

"The mind is everything. What you think you become." – Buddha

MAKE IT HAPPEN

DATE: ___/___/___

think positive

"A journey of a thousand miles must begin with a single step." – Lao Tzu

DATE:___/___/___

"Try and fail, but don't fail to try" — Anonymous

BELIEVE YOU CAN

DATE: ___/___/___

think positive

"A diamond is a chunk of coal that made good under pressure" — Anonymous

DATE: ___/___/___

"You risk more when you don't take any risks"

BELIEVE IN YOURSELF

DATE: ___/___/___

think positive

"Remember yesterday, dream of tomorrow, but live for today" — Anonymous

DATE: ___/___/___

"Wherever you go, go with all your heart" – Confucius

TAKE ACTION!

DATE:___/___/___

think positive

"Dream is not what you see in sleep, dream is the thing which does not let you sleep" — *Anonymous*

DATE:___/___/___

"All our tomorrows depend on today" — *Anonymous*

DATE:___/___/___

think positive

"Don't be pushed by your problems.
Be led by your dreams" — Anonymous

DATE: ___/___/___

"Dreams give purpose to your life and meaning to your existence"

MAKE IT HAPPEN

DATE: ___/___/___

think positive

"Once you have a dream put all your heart and soul to achieve it"

DATE: ___/___/___

"Follow your heart and your dreams will come true" – Anonymous

BELIEVE YOU CAN

DATE: ___/___/___

think positive

"You create your life by following your dreams with decisive actions"

DATE:___/___/___

"Without dreams you lose interest in life; you have no energy to move forward"

BELIEVE IN YOURSELF

DATE:___/___/___

think positive

"The road to success is always full of surprises
and temporary failures, real success comes
to those who persist and enjoy the journey"

DATE:___/___/___

"Today is another chance to get better"

TAKE ACTION!

DATE:___/___/___

think positive

"To live a creative life, we must lose our fear of being wrong" - Anonymous

DATE:___/___/___

"Believe and act as if it were impossible to fail."

DATE: ___/___/___

think positive

"Make each day count, you will never have this day again"

DATE:___/___/___

"It's not what you look at that matters, it's what you see" - Anonymous

MAKE IT HAPPEN

DATE: ___/___/___

think positive

"Successful people make a habit of doing what unsuccessful people don't want to do"
– Anonymous

DATE:___/___/___

"Nothing worth having comes easy"
- Anonymous

BELIEVE YOU CAN

DATE:___/___/___

think positive

"Be Strong! It might be stormy now, but it can't rain forever!" - Anonymous

DATE: ___/___/___

"Keep taking chances - make life a beautiful experience and never give up"

BELIEVE IN YOURSELF

WE HOPE YOU LIKED YOUR JOURNAL - NOTEBOOK
PLEASE WRITE YOUR REVIEW, IT MEANS A LOT TO US!

DESIGNED BY: Sunshine Journals Studio FOR:

CREATIVE JOURNALS FACTORY

THANK YOU!

FIND OTHER BEAUTIFUL JOURNALS, DIARIES AND NOTEBOOKS AT:

www.CreativeJournalsFactory.com

JOURNALS - DIARIES - NOTEBOOKS - COLORING BOOKS

Made in the USA
Monee, IL
13 September 2022